School of Scum Presents: Math Class
(Vulgar Arithmetic for Adults)

SCHOOL OF SCUM PRESENTS:
MATH CLASS
(VULGAR ARITHMETIC FOR ADULTS)

School of Scum Presents: Math Class
(Vulgar Arithmetic for Adults)

By
Jeremiah Mastro (Jaydaddy)

Copyright © 2025 by Jeremiah Mastro.

All rights reserved. Except for brief passages quoted in newspaper, magazine, radio, television, or online reviews, no part of this book may be reproduced in any form or by any means, electronic or mechanical, including photocopying or recording, or by information storage or retrieval system, without permission in writing from the publisher.

Published in the United States by Viva Editions, an imprint of Start Midnight, LLC, 221 River Street, Ninth Floor, Hoboken, New Jersey 07030.

Printed in the United States

Cover design: Jennifer Stimson Design
Cover image: Jeremiah Mastro, Shutterstock/XAOC, iStock/thumb
Illustrations: Louis Philippe Brunet
Text design: Westchester Publishing Services

First Edition.

10 9 8 7 6 5 4 3 2 1

Trade paper ISBN: 978-1-63228-105-0

E-book ISBN: 978-1-63228-111-1

THIS BOOK BELONGS TO

_____

_____

_____

Standard Measurements of Length		
1 ft.	=	12 in.
1 yd.	=	36 in.
1 yd.	=	3 ft.
1 mi.	=	5280 ft.
Metric Measurements of Length		
1 cm	=	10 mm
1 m	=	100 cm
1 km	=	1000 m
Metric to Standard Conversions		
1 mm	=	0.04 in.
1 cm	=	0.40 in.
1 m	=	39.4 in.
1 m	=	3.3 ft.
1 m	=	1.1 yd.
1 km	=	1093.6 yd.
1 km	=	0.62 mi.
Standard to Metric Conversions		
1 in.	=	2.54 cm
1 ft.	=	30.48 cm
1 yd.	=	91.4 cm
1 yd.	=	0.91 m
1 mi.	=	1609.34 m
1 mi.	=	1.6 km

Liquid Measurements				
1 cup	=	8 fl. oz.		
1 pint	=	2 cups	=	16 fl. oz.
1 quart	=	2 pints	=	32 fl. oz.
1 gallon	=	4 quarts	=	128 fl. oz.
Measurements of Time				
60 sec.	=	1 min.		
60 min.	=	1 hr.		
24 hrs.	=	1 day		
7 days	=	1 week		
4 weeks	=	1 month		
12 months	=	1 year		
52 weeks	=	1 year		
365 days	=	1 year		

A Note from Your Teacher

As the great Albert Einstein once said, "We cannot solve our problems with the same thinking we used when we created them." I don't really know what the fuck that means but I think it works. Instead of scrolling on your phone into a depressing pit of despair, you decided to pick up a book and learn something for once. For that, I am proud of you. If you didn't get the memo before opening the book, here's your final warning! This workbook is not for the weak. If you're offended by its innovative mathematical material at any given point in time, I advise you to close the book, take a break, and remove the tampon from your pussy. It takes a true genius like myself to understand how revolutionary this shit is. I, Mr. Peters, your teacher, am a fucking pioneer! It's finally time to give the traditional education system a run for its money. The school board can kiss my fucking ass! With that being said, it's now time to sharpen those math skills and test your morals, but remember, you need something to write with! So, take your hand out of your pants, pick up the nearest No. 2 pencil, and get to work! Oh! And <u>NO CHEATING</u>! There's an answer key in the back so you can grade yourself after you finish. Good luck, scumbag!

School of Scum Presents: Math Class 1

1. You're in a horror movie and the killer is chasing after you with a knife. There are 13 doors in the house from which you're trying to escape. There's a front-door exit and a back-door exit. What is the probability you find either exit?

   A) 1/15
   B) 2/15
   C) 2/13
   D) You're not in a horror movie, it's just your grandfather having another PTSD flashback from Vietnam.

2. If Stacy has chlamydia, how many threesomes will it take for Stacy to transmit chlamydia to 132 individuals?

   A) 48
   B) 75
   C) 66
   D) 34

2   School of Scum Presents: Math Class

3. Jaydaddy is the funniest guy on the internet. He has no competition. Everyone else is trash compared to him. Some people call him the "King of Comedy." If Jaydaddy gains 100,000 subscribers for every 20 videos he uploads, how many videos will he need to reach 1 million subscribers?

A) 300
B) 225
C) 200
D) 150

4. Nathan got a bank loan of $100,000 to start up his small business idea. He got drunk as fuck the night after, hopped on his computer, and lost $87,500 playing online roulette. I forgot to mention Nathan has a crippling gambling addiction. He shouldn't have access to money. Nathan has $12,500 left. If he bets $12,500 every spin, how many roulette spins will it take for Nathan to break even?

A) 7. He won't win, he'll lose it all.
B) 8. He won't win, he'll lose it all.
C) 6. He won't win, he'll lose it all.
D) 5. He won't win, he'll lose it all.

School of Scum Presents: Math Class 3

5. Benjamin is a discord moderator for a channel called "Planet of the Incels." Benjamin jerks off 9 times a day. In a year, how many nuts will Benjamin bust?

A) 3,285
B) 1,340
C) 876
D) 2,789

6. Jessica has irritable bowel syndrome. She takes 12 shits a day. That's 4,380 shits per year. If Jessica cures her IBS, she should be taking around 1,095 shits per year; how many shits would Jessica be taking per day?

A) 15
B) 6
C) 3
D) 1

School of Scum Presents: Math Class

7. Jeffrey, the local crackhead, has 27 8-balls on him. Jeffrey falls asleep on a bench and wakes up with 13 8-balls. He was either robbed or he used that shit, he can't remember. How many 8-balls did Jeffrey (possibly) go through?

A) 10
B) 7
C) 14
D) 23

8. Gary likes being pegged by his girlfriend, Letty. One night, the strap-on breaks, and now the peg is stuck inside Gary's ass. Instead of calling an ambulance, Letty and Gary drive to the hospital. Letty is speeding on the highway at 120 mph. Before getting to the hospital, they get pulled over by police. If the officer tells Letty she's driving 50 mph over the speed limit, what is the speed limit?

A) 50 mph
B) 80 mph
C) 70 mph
D) 120 mph

School of Scum Presents: Math Class 5

9. If Betsy has a body count of 110 bodies, and in the next week she adds 17 bodies, how many bodies in total does Betsy have?

   A) 196
   B) 127
   C) 264
   D) None of the above. She's a virgin.

10. Danny and his friends are playing hopscotch. Danny had his left leg amputated after a shark attack. If Danny only has one leg, how many hops would it take for Danny to finish the hopscotch course?

   A) 12
   B) 6
   C) 11
   D) None of the above. He can't play.

6   School of Scum Presents: Math Class

11. If Jake can fit 20 cocks in his mouth, and 5 men remove their cocks from his mouth, how many cocks are left in Jake's mouth?

A) 20
B) 16
C) 15
D) 10

12. Tabitha is a petty thief, and shoplifts on the regular. She went to the store and stole a cucumber ($1.05), lubricant ($8.95), and a douche ($15.99). An employee named Darius, who is 6'6", weighs 301 lbs., and used to play middle linebacker in college, saw her stuff the 3 items into her pants. He sprints at her, and runs through her like a fucking Mack truck. Tabitha is now hospitalized and handcuffed to the bed, recovering from her injuries. If Tabitha had gotten away with stealing the items, how much money in product would she have stolen?

A) $22.50
B) $19.05
C) $25.99
D) $34.95

13. Trevor is a drug dealer. He has 6 kilos of meth in a bag for a drug deal that's going down. One kilo is equivalent to 2.2 lbs. Before handing over the drugs for the money, the leader Esteban Quiñones holds him at gunpoint and says, "You done fucked up, pendejo." Quiñones takes 2 kilos out of Trevor's bag. The police come out of nowhere, making a surprise drug bust! Trevor runs away, evading the cops. He is now left with 4 kilos of meth. What percentage of meth did Trevor lose?

    A) 33.33%
    B) 50%
    C) 66.66%
    D) 0%. The cops arrested Quiñones and gave Trevor his drugs back.

14. Emily is a basic white bitch. Her favorite drink from the coffee shop is a large iced white mocha, with sweet cream cold foam, and extra caramel drizzle on top. Emily buys it every single day. Her drink costs $8.47. In a year, how much has Emily spent on coffee?

    A) $2,056.65
    B) $8,470.99
    C) $1,673.50
    D) $3,091.55

8 School of Scum Presents: Math Class

15. How many words are in this dialogue?

"Go fuck yourself, Dad! You can't just walk back into my life! You found out that I'm a gay camboy model making five hundred thousand dollars a year and now you show up!? A little late, don't ya think? Go get a handout from someone else!"

A) 46
B) 27
C) 32
D) 50

16. Lester and Sandra have been a couple for 5 years. Lester is now 67 years old and Sandra is now 23 years old. How old was Sandra when she and Lester got together?

A) 21
B) 20
C) 19
D) 18. Lester's a sick fuck.

School of Scum Presents: Math Class 9

17. Since 18 years of age, Daniel has had 3 imaginary friends. For every year that Daniel ages, he adds 3 more imaginary friends. Daniel is now 30 years old. How many imaginary friends does Daniel have in total?

A) 65
B) 45
C) 23
D) 39. Daniel has chronic schizophrenia.

18. You're taking a shit at your grandmother's house. You're 15 minutes into your shit when you realize there is no toilet paper. The only thing you can do is yell at your grandma to get you some. Grandma doesn't have her hearing aids in so she's deaf as fuck. In her supply closet, she has toilet paper, cotton swabs, maxi pads, sandpaper, duct tape, and some pills. Out of all the items, what is the probability grandma heard you correctly and brings you the **toilet paper**?

A) 1/6
B) 1/5
C) 1/7
D) 2/7. Sandpaper works just fine.

10 School of Scum Presents: Math Class

19. Eddy is practicing a new jelqing method. Jelqing is a technique used by individuals to enlarge their penis. Eddy stretches his penis 4 times from base to head, then twists his mushroom tip 2 times counterclockwise, and 2 times clockwise. He repeats the process 30 times every jelqing session. If Eddy's 3-inch micropenis grows to his goal of 5 inches, how many centimeters has Eddy grown?

   A) 2.54 cm
   B) 3.14 cm
   C) 5.08 cm
   D) 5.30 cm

20. What are the 3 shapes that create this image?

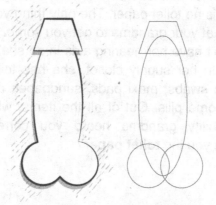

   A) Oval, sphere, and square
   B) Circle, oval, and trapezoid
   C) Square, rectangle, and trapezoid
   D) Diamond, triangle, and circle

School of Scum Presents: Math Class   11

21. How many words are in this dialogue?

"Grandma! Where the fuck are my chocolate chip cookies!? You said you were making them an hour ago. You keep this shit up, I'll tell Mom to put you back in the nursing home."

A) 34
B) 27
C) 29
D) 40

22. You're playing tag with your little brother, and he finally gets you. Enraged, you grab him by the neck and throw him into the fucking wall. The impact makes 4 holes in the wall. Each hole costs the same to repair. If the grand total for repairs is $1,255.68, how much did each hole cost to repair?

A) $313.92
B) $125.67
C) $1,255.67
D) $355.67

12   School of Scum Presents: Math Class

23. How many words are in Tyler's poem?

It was never a phase, Mom!
My heart is a ticking time bomb.
I black my eyes to hide in a shroud of darkness.
I have no control, someone put me in a harness.
My soul is an empty void of despair.
You gave birth to a lost child, a child who will never care.

A) 23
B) 55
C) 40
D) 56

24. Alyssa has a mukbang channel. She made a huge following by stuffing her face with food all day. Alyssa films 3 videos per day, averaging around 70,000 likes per post. On top of the 1 million total likes her page has, how many videos will it take for her to reach her goal of 10 million likes?

A) 76
B) 97
C) 129
D) 106

School of Scum Presents: Math Class   13

25. The police caught Jay parking in a handicap spot. This is the first time he's been caught. He's been charged with a $250 fine. If Jay had been caught the other 768 times he's parked in a handicap spot, how much would Jay have had to pay?

A) $90,000
B) $250,000
C) $110,000
D) $192,000

26. Mike pulled a prank on his best friend Harry. When Harry wasn't looking, Mike hit him over the head with a hammer and threw him off the second-story balcony. Harry is now in the hospital with 2 broken legs and a fractured skull. Mike bought a candy bar ($2.50), a bag of ranch tortilla chips ($3.50), and a can of diet soda ($3) from the hospital vending machine. How much did Mike spend on snacks?

A) $6.50
B) $10.50
C) $8
D) $9. Mike is now serving 30 years in prison for attempted murder.

14   School of Scum Presents: Math Class

27. The human brain has approximately 86 billion brain cells. If Jimmy is missing 95% of his brain cells, how many brain cells does Jimmy have?

   A) 50,000,000,000. Jimmy is special.
   B) 43,000,000,000. Jimmy is really special.
   C) 8,600,000,000. Jimmy is really, really special.
   D) 4,300,000,000. Jimmy is really, really, really special.

28. Billy is in timeout. He defiantly shit all over the backseat of his parent's car because they didn't take him out for fast food. Billy's parents put him in timeout for 1 hour. How many seconds did Billy sit in timeout?

   A) 3,600 seconds
   B) 600 seconds
   C) 6,000 seconds
   D) 1,600 seconds

School of Scum Presents: Math Class 15

29. Devin struggles with sleep paralysis. An armed robber breaks into Devin's house in the middle of the night. Devin sees the robber, but is constrained to his bed. After taking a fat shit in Devin's bathroom, the robber proceeds to steal Devin's $300 TV, $500 gaming console, $1,100 laptop, $700 tablet, and his $450 limited edition turbo-suck pocket pussy. If the robber pawns each item for half of its original price, how much will the robber make in total?

A) $3,050
B) $1,525
C) $2,140
D) $950

30. This is Devin's turbo-suck pocket pussy. Solve for X.

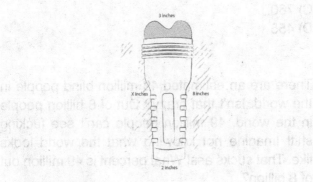

A) 7 inches
B) 6 inches
C) 8 inches
D) None of the above

16　School of Scum Presents: Math Class

31. You're in physical education class, and no one ran the full mile. The PE teacher sits everyone down for a motivational lecture:

"When you wake up tomorrow to brush your teeth, I want you to look in the mirror and tell that fat fuck across from you that you're disgusted . . . You're disgusted at what you've become. Heart disease is right around the corner, Fatty! Keep stuffing that face with pizza and ice cream and you'll be in an early grave! Love you guys. Let's do better next time."

After the motivational lecture, he tells everyone in the class to give him 15 push-ups. There are 35 kids in the class. How many push-ups are completed in total?

A) 350
B) 525
C) 760
D) 455

32. There are an estimated 49 million blind people in the world. Isn't that crazy? Out of 8 billion people in the world, 49 million people can't see fucking shit! Imagine not knowing what the world looks like. That sucks ass! What percent is 49 million out of 8 billion?

A) 4.9%
B) 1%
C) Less than 1%
D) 8.49%

School of Scum Presents: Math Class   17

33. Ryan, Kenny, Tanner, and Preston are best friends. They have a group chat where they discuss pretty wild shit. "I think we should start a podcast!" Preston tells the boys. "Let's do it!" Tanner agrees. Each of them takes out a loan for $25,000. In total, they spend $100,000 for a studio, equipment, and a hefty advertising budget. One year after the start of their podcast, they have generated $2.75 in revenue. They all accept that their podcast idea was a miserable failure and now each of them are $25,000 in debt. With a payment of $500 a month each, how many months will it take to pay off their debt?

A) 50
B) 25
C) 55
D) 20

34. How many words are in Tyler's poem?

This world is a cesspool for the wicked.
There's a million crimes in my head that I haven't committed.
But if you push me to the brink,
I'll make sure the human race is extinct.
I foam at the mouth like a rabid animal,
I hate my own kind, they call me a cannibal.

A) 20
B) 54
C) 75
D) 33

18   School of Scum Presents: Math Class

35. Your boys' group chat was leaked and now you're in the principal's office going through the text messages.

Cameron: *I wonder what Ms. Riviera's fart-box tastes like.*
Kyle: *Our Spanish teacher?*
Cameron: *Yes. I want to taste that brown chili ring.*

Cameron has now been suspended from school for one month. If Cameron has Spanish class on Tuesdays, Thursdays, and Fridays, how many times will Cameron miss Spanish class during his suspension?

A) 15
B) 7
C) 16
D) 12

36. Your unemployed friend sends you approximately 50 social reels a day. If you only watch 5 of them per day, how many reels have gone unwatched in a month, assuming there are 31 days in each?

A) 565
B) 780
C) 956
D) 1,395. Tell your friend to get a life.

School of Scum Presents: Math Class   19

37. You finally meet your friend's baby, and it's ugly as fuck. "Isn't she adorable!?" your friend asks. You don't want to say the wrong thing and hurt your friend's feelings, so you have to lie. Out of all the responses below, what is the probability you respond politely?

"What the fuck is that!?"
"Does it bite?"
"She's beautiful, I'm so happy for you!"
"Why's it looking at me like that?"
"Kinda looks like Gollum."
"What a cutie pie!"

A) 2/5
B) 1/6
C) 2/6
D) 3/6

38. Nicholas is on a road trip with his family. They're traveling from Florida to New York. His bitch sister won't stop complaining about how long the drive is taking, his mom is telling her to shut the fuck up, and his dad's playing pocket pool with his left hand while steering with his right. At this point, Nicholas wants to throw himself out of the car going 90 mph on the highway. The family trip is 1,250 miles in total. If the family's car gets 32 miles per gallon on the highway, how many gallons of gas do they use for the road trip in total?

A) 35.7 gallons
B) 50 gallons
C) 39 gallons
D) 41.7 gallons

20　School of Scum Presents: Math Class

39. Missy has 34 dildos, 14 butt plugs, and 6 pairs of anal beads. Missy wants to downsize because she does not have enough room to store her toys. If Missy throws away half the amount of each toy she has, how many toys will Missy have in total?

A) 17
B) 27
C) 8
D) 24

40. Take a look at Missy's anal beads.

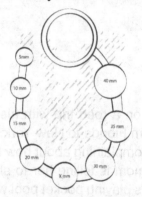

There are exactly 8 beads with the first bead starting at 5 mm and the last bead ending at 40 mm. Solve for X.

A) 50 mm
B) 24 mm
C) 35 mm
D) None of the above

School of Scum Presents: Math Class   21

41. It's New Year's! Your resolution is to take the gym seriously after being a fat fuck for the holidays. Every year you tell yourself the same shit and then you cancel your gym membership by the end of February. You pathetic pussy. If you hit the gym Monday through Friday for 8 weeks before you quit, how many days do you go to the gym?

A) 35
B) 50
C) 20
D) 40

42. Larry is an insomniac. The motherfucker can't sleep. He's missed 2 nights of sleep a week for the past year. In 52 weeks, how many nights of sleep does Larry miss in total?

A) 45
B) 67
C) 104
D) 96

22   School of Scum Presents: Math Class

43. Tara became a raging alcoholic after her breakup with Ron. She drowns herself in 4 bottles of wine a night while sobbing to romantic comedies, envying the actors' onscreen relationships. Just 5 months later, she meets a new boyfriend and cleans herself up. How many bottles of wine did Tara drink in those 5 months, assuming there are 31 days in each?

A) 550
B) 465
C) 700
D) 620

44. How many words are in Tyler's poem?

My blood is cold like ice.
Get on my bad side, and I might not be so nice.
Demons live in my head rent free,
but no one will ever free ME.
Free me from this darkness, free me from my shadows.
I'm a bad man, send me to the gallows.

A) 56
B) 73
C) 51
D) 45

School of Scum Presents: Math Class   23

45. Frank has a serious porn addiction. He loves all kinds of porn: PAWG, BBW, MILF, Mature, and even the occasional BBC porn. Frank's browser history shows that he watches around 950 videos a week. If there are 52 weeks in a year and Frank keeps this up, how many videos will he end up watching in one year?

A) 49,400
B) 32,650
C) 27,550
D) 41,400

46. Chester is a dirty fuck. The kid doesn't shower at all. Chester takes about 2 showers a month. That's fucking disgusting. And he wonders why he's still a virgin. Maybe it's because you smell like shit, my dude! I know that ass is crusty as fuck. Chester is 30 years old. If Chester's been taking 2 showers a month since he was 15, how many showers did Chester take in those 15 years?

A) 275. Dirty bitch.
B) 360. Stinky fuck.
C) 460. Don't open your legs.
D) 500. Scrub that ass, Buddy.

24   School of Scum Presents: Math Class

47. An adult has approximately 32 teeth. By the age of 44, 69% of adults have lost at least one tooth. Timmy is 24, doesn't brush his teeth for shit, and packs dip into his bottom lip 3 times a day. His breath smells like a skunk's asshole, and his bottom teeth are rotting by the day. If there's 16 bottom teeth in the adult mouth, and 7 have already fallen out, how many bottom teeth does Timmy have left?

A) 8
B) 9
C) 7
D) 4

48. Jacob hates his job because the pay sucks and his manager is a smug, two-faced bitch. The kinda manager that'll tell you, "There are donuts in the break room," and then stab you in the back the second you turn around. Jacob quits his shitty job and finds a better one. He was making $8.25 an hour, and now he's making $15.50 an hour. If Jacob works 40 hours a week, how much money does he make in a month?

A) $3,040
B) $2,068
C) $2,480
D) $4,050

School of Scum Presents: Math Class

49. Benny eats 7 cheeseburgers every day. There are 500 calories in 1 cheeseburger, and 3,500 calories equate to 1 pound of fat. How many pounds of fat will Benny gain in the next 90 days?

    A) 35 lbs.
    B) 90 lbs.
    C) 300 lbs.
    D) None of the above. He'll go into cardiac arrest.

50. This is Benny's double chin.

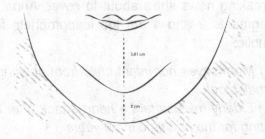

    The distance from Benny's mouth to his chin is 3.81 cm. The distance from Benny's chin to his double chin is half of that. Solve for X.

    A) 1.9 cm
    B) 1.75 cm
    C) 1.5 cm
    D) None of the above

26   School of Scum Presents: Math Class

51. There are 100 fucked-up questions in this work-book. Each question is worth 1 point. If you get a grade of 46%, how many questions did you answer incorrectly?

A) 10. Wow! An A-.
B) 20. Good job! You got a B.
C) 35. Oof! Not the best—a big fat D.
D) 54. You failed miserably. Rethink life.

52. Anna is a news reporter. There are 6 segments of breaking news she's about to cover. Anna thinks segments 2 and 4 are too inappropriate for the public:

1.) Mom saves her infant child from choking on a small block
2.) Elderly man suffers a heart attack after ejaculating for the first time in 30 years
3.) A local pizza shop catches fire after an oven malfunction
4.) Wife stabs husband 42 times after finding out he had an affair
5.) Kind police officer guides a blind woman across the street
6.) Massive pileup collision going north on the highway

If the news team cut segments 2 and 4, what percent of material was cut from the broadcast?

A) 25%
B) 33%
C) 50%
D) 44%

School of Scum Presents: Math Class 27

53. A sick kid makes a charity wish to meet his favorite superhero. The superhero actor only gets paid for 1 hour, so he's on a tight schedule. If the actor can only grant 34 wishes out of 125, what percent of wishes did he make come true?

A) 34%
B) 20%
C) 55%
D) 27%

54. Blake had 2 parents, but he lost his dad in a car accident. How many parents does Blake have left?

A) 0
B) 1
C) 2
D) 3

28   School of Scum Presents: Math Class

55. Bridgette wanted some DSLs. She got filler injections to plump up her lips. The average lip filler injection is around 0.5 to 2 mL of synthetic hyaluronic acid. The doctor fucked up and accidentally used twice the average dose. He injected 4 mL into her lips and now she looks botched as fuck. What is the equivalent to 4 milliliters in liters?

A) 0.004 L
B) 0.040 L
C) 0.400 L
D) 0.002 L

56. Monique wants to go to a hip-hop concert with her 3 friends. It's $1,125 for each front-row ticket. Monique's boyfriend Ricky tries to talk her out of it, saying she should save the money. She breaks up with her boyfriend because she's an independent bad bitch that don't need no man. After calling Ricky "a broke-ass bum," she storms out of his house, calls her friends, and purchases 4 tickets, for which her friends will pay her back after the concert. How much did Monique spend for all 4 tickets?

A) $3,750
B) $5,000
C) $4,365
D) $4,500. Her friends didn't pay her back, so now she's a broke-ass bum.

School of Scum Presents: Math Class   29

57. Tessa uses Snapchat almost every day. Her Snapscore is approximately 370,000, which means she's really popular on the app. When she was with her boyfriend Travis, her Snapscore was only around 18,500. A year after they broke up, her Snapscore skyrocketed to 370,000. How many times did her original score multiply for Tessa to reach a score of 370,000?

A) 5
B) 10
C) 16
D) 20. She's a thot.

58. Bruce is going Black Friday shopping to get a new TV. The store only has 1 TV that he wants. It was originally priced at $1,600, and is now on sale for $950! The minute the store opens their doors, the crowd goes nuts. Rushing to the electronics section, Bruce trips an old lady, backhands some pregnant bitch, and punt kicks a woman's child like a football so she runs in the opposite direction. Bruce successfully secures the TV and makes his purchase. How much money does Bruce save with the Black Friday deal?

A) $700
B) $850
C) $650
D) $1,000

30   School of Scum Presents: Math Class

59. Dexter is going bald. His hairline is absolutely fucked. He's flying to Turkey next week to get a hair transplant. One hair graft has around 4 follicles. Dexter needs 3,000 hair grafts to have a full head of hair again. How many follicles should Dexter have after his transplant?

A) 12,000
B) 6,000
C) 9,000
D) 15,000

60. This is Dexter's hairline before flying to Turkey for his hair transplant.

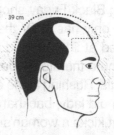

As you can see, his hairline is completely pushed back. The distance from his original hairline to his neck hairline is 39 cm. If the distance of his recession is 1/3 of that, how far did Dexter's hairline recede?

A) 19.5 cm
B) 13 cm
C) 9 cm
D) 13.5 cm

School of Scum Presents: Math Class   31

61. You're 8 years old again and it's Christmas morning. Santa ate all the cookies you put out for him last night. Your Christmas list had exactly 34 items on it but there's only 27 presents under the tree. How many presents did Santa forget?

A) 4
B) 10
C) 8
D) 7. Santa's a good-for-nothing son of a bitch. Fat fuck forgot my presents but didn't forget to eat those cookies.

62. Phil is playing blackjack at the casino and he's down bad. The dealer beats Phil the tenth time in a row. Phil threatens to rip the dealer's cock off and feed it to him. Phil is now banned from the casino. Before he was escorted out, Phil had 4 $25 chips, 7 $5 chips, and 15 $2 chips. How much money are the chips worth in total?

A) $165
B) $88
C) $250
D) $55

32   School of Scum Presents: Math Class

63. It's little Baxter's bedtime. Baxter counts 67 sheep before falling asleep and another 34 sheep in his dream. His dream suddenly turns into a nightmare when 18 sheep get flattened by a fucking semi-truck. How many sheep in total were in Baxter's dream, including his nightmare?

A) 101
B) 52
C) 67
D) 18

64. Lori is a college student who just found out she failed her final exams. Lori studied 7 days a week, and each day she took 40 mg of a "study buddy" to stay focused. How many milligrams of the "study buddy" did Lori take in total?

A) 80 mg
B) 160 mg
C) 240 mg
D) 280 mg. She should try cocaine next time.

65. Caleb and Sasha are getting ready to go on a double date with their friends. Caleb takes 10 minutes to get ready while Sasha takes 2 hours and 15 minutes to get ready. What's the difference in minutes that Caleb and Sasha take to get ready?

A) 70 minutes
B) 65 minutes
C) 100 minutes
D) 125 minutes. Being a girl fucking sucks.

66. Whitney's car is falling apart. On top of all the other car problems, the blinker lights are now dead. Whitney's car takes approximately 14 oz. of blinker fluid while other cars take around 9 oz. What's the difference in blinker fluid?

A) 5 oz.
B) 7 oz.
C) 9 oz.
D) There's no such thing as blinker fluid, you fucking idiot.

34   School of Scum Presents: Math Class

67. Keith is a survivalist. When he's not doomsday prepping, he challenges Mother Nature. Keith travels to a remote wilderness in the winter where it's –60°F. He tries camping overnight in his tent, but can't start a fire. Before dying from hypothermia, Keith is emergency airlifted to safety. What is –60°F in Celsius?

A) –60°
B) –51.1°. Keith is a shitty survivalist who doesn't even know how to start a fire.
C) –59.5°
D) –6.0°. Temperature is science, not math!

68. Vanessa is a supermodel. She's getting ready for a huge photoshoot but she weighs 16 more pounds than she'd like. Vanessa eats 1 meal per day, and right after eating she forces herself to throw up. With this method, she loses about 1.6 lbs. per day. How many days will it take for Vanessa to shed 16 lbs.?

A) 7
B) 8
C) 9
D) 10. Vanessa is bulimic.

69. Peter Pissman is practicing a revolutionary hydration protocol. Peter recycles the water he drinks throughout the day by drinking his own urine. If Peter drinks 32 cups of his own piss per day, how many gallons of piss did he drink in 762 days?

   A) 1,524 gallons
   B) 762 gallons
   C) 3,467 gallons
   D) 1,245 gallons

70. Take a look at Peter Pissman's 2 L piss-bottle.

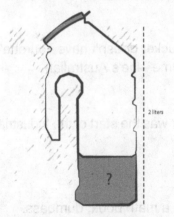

   If Peter drank 75% of his own piss, how many milliliters of piss is left inside Peter's piss bottle?

   A) 0.50 mL
   B) 1.25 mL
   C) 200 mL
   D) 500 mL

36   School of Scum Presents: Math Class

71. Tucker has Tourette's syndrome. He says the word
    "cunt" approximately 97 times per day. How many
    times does Tucker say "cunt" in 2 weeks?

    A) 679
    B) 1,358
    C) 2,154
    D) 970. Tucker doesn't have Tourette's
       syndrome—he's Australian.

72. What year was the start of the Industrial Revolution?

    A) 1650
    B) 1905
    C) 1500
    D) This is a math book, dumbass.

School of Scum Presents: Math Class   37

73. Johnny was born with a congenital hand deformity. He has 3 fingers on one hand and 4 fingers on the other. Johnny's friend has a pit bull named Brock. Brock mistakenly used Johnny's hand as a chew toy, causing Johnny to lose 2 fingers. How many fingers does Johnny now have in total?

A) 10
B) 7
C) 15
D) 5

74. Jerry drinks 12 cans of diet soda per day. Each can has approximately 184 mg of aspartame, a low-calorie artificial sweetener, in it. If Jerry drinks 12 cans of diet soda per day, how many milligrams of aspartame is he consuming in 365 days?

A) 345,765 mg
B) 750,560 mg
C) 97,864 mg
D) 805,920 mg. Jerry's gonna get cancer.

38 School of Scum Presents: Math Class

75. Carrie had A-cup titties. She upgraded to a B cup, but now she wants D cups. She's upgrading from a 200-cc implant to a 600-cc implant. What's the difference in cubic centimeters?

A) 100 cc
B) 200 cc
C) 300 cc
D) 400 cc. Go big or go home.

76. Harold is a competitive eater. He comes in first place every year at his town's annual hot dog eating competition. Last year, the eaters had to inhale 10 hot dogs with no bun, as fast as they could. This year, they increased the number of hot dogs to 20. Harold uses a method where he shoves all the hot dogs in his mouth at once. He got 17 girthy wieners inside his stretched mouth, but before he could chew, 4 of them slipped down his throat, causing him to choke to death. Not including the 4 lodged in his throat, how many girthy wieners did Harold have in his mouth?

A) 17
B) 15
C) 9
D) 13. Imagine dying because you choked on 4 girthy meat sticks—that blows, no pun intended.

School of Scum Presents: Math Class 39

77. You and your girlfriend are on a game show and you have the chance to win exactly $5 million. The rules are simple. A kick to the dick is worth $20,000, and a punch to the tit is worth $5,000. You have 5 minutes to reach the maximum amount of $5 million. If you let your girlfriend kick you in the dick every time, how many kicks to the dick will it take for you to win $5 million?

A) 500
B) 250
C) 300
D) 200

78. In the United Kingdom alone, approximately 4 billion tampons are discarded each year. The number of used tampons in the UK per year is around half the human population! How many used tampons will there be in the UK after 7 years?

A) 47 billion
B) 4 trillion
C) 28 million
D) 28 billion. Bloody hell! Fucking twats!

40   School of Scum Presents: Math Class

79. If you thought the United Kingdom was bad, wait until you hear about the United States. In the US alone, approximately 7 billion tampons are discarded each year. The number of used tampons in the US per year is almost the same number as the human population! How many used tampons will there be in the US after 7 years?

   A) 7 trillion
   B) 77 billion
   C) 49 million
   D) 49 billion. Periods are fucking gross.

80. What are the two shapes that create this image?

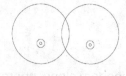

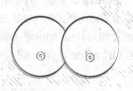

   A) Circle and hexagon
   B) Octagon and circle
   C) Square and circle
   D) Diamond and oval

School of Scum Presents: Math Class 41

81. There are 7 babies on a plane and 3 of them start crying before takeoff. If you open the emergency exit and throw those 3 babies out of the plane, how many babies are left?

A) 2
B) 3
C) 4
D) 5

82. If there are 17.6 million double orphans (a child who has lost both parents) worldwide, out of those orphans, how many dead parents are there?

A) 35.2 million
B) 56.5 million
C) 24.8 million
D) 111.6 million

42   School of Scum Presents: Math Class

83. Bubbles is a stripper. Her shift is from 8:00 p.m. to 2:00 a.m. and she makes $10 an hour. On top of her hourly wage, she made $376 in tips because she wouldn't stop shaking that big bubbly ass. How much money did Bubbles make?

A) $436
B) $386
C) $765
D) $450

84. Reggie's wife Fiona was pissed at him for playing games with the boys. Fiona started bitching at 7:45 p.m. and then stopped bitching 1 hour and 27 minutes later. At what time did Fiona stop bitching?

A) 9:12 p.m.
B) 8:55 p.m.
C) 9:22 p.m.
D) 8:57 p.m.

School of Scum Presents: Math Class   43

85. Monica hates that her husband Terry doesn't last long enough in bed. Terry was balls deep in his wife at 9:32 p.m. and finished at 9:36 p.m. How long did Terry last?

A) 3 minutes
B) 5 minutes
C) 4 minutes
D) 2 minutes

86. Josie is a pasty white bitch, so she went to the beach to get her tan on. She forgot her sunscreen, but it didn't matter because she was only planning to tan for 30 minutes. Josie fell asleep on her towel at 11:25 a.m. and woke up 5 hours and 7 minutes later. What time did Josie wake up?

A) 4:15 p.m.
B) 5:07 p.m.
C) 3:57 p.m.
D) 4:32 p.m. Josie has severe sun poisoning.

44   School of Scum Presents: Math Class

87. Julio has cystic acne. His face looks like a pepperoni pizza. You could play connect the dots with the constellations on his face. Each month, 8 more pimples appear. How many more pimples will Julio have in 6 months?

A) 72
B) 48
C) 56
D) 86

88. Stanley has a stutter. He has trouble every time he says the word "to." Read Stanley's sentence below:

"Are we going to the mall? I want to get that new hoodie. Then I want to get some Chinese food at the food court."

If Stanley stutters 3 times every time he says the word "to," how many times does Stanley stutter?

A) 6
B) 9
C) 3
D) 12

School of Scum Presents: Math Class 45

89. Tobin collects his own toenails. What a sick, twisted fuck. He clips his toenails every 2 weeks and collects 2 toenail clippings per toe. With his 10 toes, how many toenail clippings in total does Tobin collect in 52 weeks?

   A) 1,045
   B) 372
   C) 520
   D) 830

90. How many planets are in our solar system?

   A) 7
   B) 6
   C) 9. Give Pluto some love.
   D) Again, this is a math book!

46   School of Scum Presents: Math Class

91. You're in prison taking a shower and you accidentally drop the soap. Before you bend down to grab it, you scan the area. There are 5 guys in the showers with you. You play it safe and decide to leave the soap on the floor. All 5 guys end up leaving the showers after you didn't take the bait. What percent of guys left the showers?

A) 95%
B) 80%
C) 50%
D) 100%. You saved your ass, literally.

92. George is constipated as fuck. He's sitting on the toilet trying to release a fat shit. George sits on the toilet at 9:45 a.m. After 2 hours and 16 minutes, he finally empties his bowels. What time does George get off the toilet?

A) 10:59 a.m.
B) 12:31 p.m.
C) 11:34 a.m.
D) 12:01 p.m. George has 2 new hemorrhoids.

School of Scum Presents: Math Class   47

93. Lucas and Roger play college football. They go to the locker room to measure each other's cocks for fun. Lucas is 4 inches and Roger is 7 inches. Using > (greater than) or < (less than), which answer is correct?

A) 4 < 7
B) 4 > 7
C) 7 < 4
D) None of the above

94. I buy a bag of chips expecting 5 servings. When I open the bag, half of it is full of fucking air! As you can tell, I'm pretty fucking pissed right now. I'm writing this as I'm eating a bag of air. If 50% of the bag is empty as fuck, how many servings of chips are there?

A) 2.5
B) 3
C) 2.75
D) 1

48   School of Scum Presents: Math Class

95. Abigail and her husband want to adopt conjoined twin brothers. Approximately 70% of conjoined twins are female. If 70% are female, how many are male?

    A) 40%
    B) 35%
    C) 25%
    D) 30%. Buy one, get one free.

96. Mario is a pizza delivery driver working the late-night shift. He's delivering an extra-large pepperoni pizza to a woman named Mia. As Mario walks up the front stairs, he trips and eats shit because Mia didn't put the porch light on. He checks the pizza and sees that 17 pepperoni slices fell off. If there were 38 pepperoni slices in total, how many are left on the pizza?

    A) 22
    B) 21
    C) 15
    D) 16

School of Scum Presents: Math Class   49

97. There are 27 kids on the school bus. Among them, 9 didn't put their seat belts on because they're stubborn little shits. The bus driver, Eugene, had a little too much to drink before his shift. He hits a speed bump at 50 mph and the 9 kids launch into the air like fucking rag dolls. What fraction of kids didn't have their seat belts on?

A) ½
B) ⅔
C) ⅓
D) 2/4

98. Your ex-girlfriend is batshit crazy. At dinner, she stabs you in the hand with a knife because you smiled at the server. The cops are called, and they determine that your ex-girlfriend is a danger to herself. They put her in a straitjacket and throw her in a padded cell shaped like a cube. A cube has six sides. If the ceiling is too high, how many walls, including the floor, can the crazy bitch bounce off of?

A) 5
B) 6
C) 3
D) 2

50   School of Scum Presents: Math Class

99. Shirley and Mandy are arguing about who has bigger tits. Shirley's rocking a pair of D-cup titties while Mandy has H-cup cannons. Using > (greater than) or < (less than), which answer is correct?

A) D > H
B) H < D
C) D < H
D) None of the above

100. You've made it to question 100! Congrats! What is $3.14 \times 1,3019234/12347 \times 8 + 13 - 1804351 \times 235 - 135425 \times 2\ 105 + 1 - 1243818723847 = ?$

A) –1.247650876
B) 2.456097
C) –3,1456780082
D) None of the above are correct, because even I don't know the fucking answer.

I SAID NO CHEATING, SCUMBAG! BUT IF YOU ARE HERE TO ACTUALLY REVIEW YOUR ANSWERS, THEY ARE ON THE NEXT PAGE . . .

Answer Key
(Time to Count... Again)

1. C (2/13)
2. C (66)
3. C (200)
4. B (8. He won't win, he'll lose it all.)
5. A (3,285)
6. C (3)
7. C (14)
8. C (70 mph)
9. B (127)
10. D (None of the above. He can't play.)
11. C (15)
12. C ($25.99)
13. A (33.33%)
14. D ($3,091.55)
15. A (46)
16. D (18. Lester's a sick fuck.)
17. D (39. Daniel has chronic schizophrenia.)
18. A (1/6)
19. C (5.08 cm)
20. B (Circle, oval, and trapezoid)
21. A (34)
22. A ($313.92)
23. B (55)

School of Scum Presents: Math Class 53

24. C (129)
25. D ($192,000)
26. D ($9. Mike is now serving 30 years in prison for attempted murder.)
27. D (4,300,000,000. Jimmy is really, really, really special.)
28. A (3,600)
29. B ($1,525)
30. C (8 inches)
31. B (525)
32. C (Less than 1%)
33. A (50)
34. B (54)
35. D (12)
36. D (1,395. Tell your friend to get a life.)
37. C (2/6)
38. C (39 gallons)
39. B (27)
40. D (None of the above)
41. D (40)
42. C (104)
43. D (620)
44. C (51)
45. A (49,400)
46. B (360. Stinky fuck.)
47. B (9)
48. C ($2,480)
49. B (90 lbs.)
50. A (1.9 cm)
51. D (54. You failed miserably. Rethink life.)
52. B (33%)
53. D (27%)

54 School of Scum Presents: Math Class

54. B (1)
55. A (0.004 L)
56. D ($4,500. Her friends didn't pay her back, so now she's a broke-ass bum.)
57. D (20. She's a thot.)
58. C ($650)
59. A (12,000)
60. B (13 cm)
61. D (7. Santa's a good-for-nothing son of a bitch. Fat fuck forgot my presents but didn't forget to eat those cookies.)
62. A ($165)
63. B (52)
64. D (280 mg. She should try cocaine next time.)
65. D (125 minutes. Being a girl fucking sucks.)
66. D (There's no such thing as blinker fluid, you fucking idiot.)
67. B (–51.1°. Keith is a shitty survivalist who doesn't even know how to start a fire.)
68. D (10. Vanessa is bulimic.)
69. A (1,524 gallons)
70. D (500 mL)
71. B (1,358)
72. D (This is a math book, dumbass.)
73. D (5)
74. D (805,920 mg. Jerry's gonna get cancer.)
75. D (400 cc. Go big or go home.)
76. D (13. Imagine dying because you choked on 4 girthy meat sticks—that blows, no pun intended.)
77. B (250)
78. D (28 billion. Bloody hell! Fucking twats!)
79. D (49 billion. Periods are fucking gross.)

School of Scum Presents: Math Class 55

80. B (Octagon and circle)
81. C (4)
82. A (35.2 million)
83. A ($436)
84. A (9:12 p.m.)
85. C (4 minutes)
86. D (4:32 p.m. Josie has severe sun poisoning.)
87. B (48)
88. B (9)
89. C (520)
90. D (Again, this is a math book!)
91. D (100%. You saved your ass, literally.)
92. D (12:01 p.m. George has 2 new hemorrhoids.)
93. A ($4 < 7$)
94. A (2.5)
95. D (30%. Buy one, get one free.)
96. B (21)
97. C ($\frac{1}{3}$)
98. A (5)
99. C ($D < H$)
100. D (None of the above are correct, because even I don't know the fucking answer.)

HOW'D YOU DO?

F (0% to 59%): You're a miserable FAILURE. Try again next time!

D (60% to 69%): You barely made it. Suck on this fat D!

C (70% to 79%): Needs improvement. Just like your sex life.

B (80% to 89%): Good job! How does it feel to always place second?

A (90% to 100%): The Teacher's Pet! Keep kissing my ass and you'll get a full-ride to an Ivy League!

www.ingramcontent.com/pod-product-compliance
Lightning Source LLC
Chambersburg PA
CBHW010539310725
30395CB00001B/1